Eve.

Eastern
leopard frogs
and watercress
on the koi pond

Every Species of Hope

*Georgics, Haiku, and
Other Poems*

Michael J. Rosen

with illustrations by the author

TRILLIUM, AN IMPRINT OF
THE OHIO STATE UNIVERSITY PRESS
COLUMBUS

Library of Congress Cataloging-in-Publication Data

Names: Rosen, Michael J., 1954– author.

Title: Every species of hope : georgics, haiku, and other poems / Michael J. Rosen.

Description: Columbus : Trillium, an imprint of The Ohio State University Press, [2017]

Identifiers: LCCN 2017026629 | ISBN 9780814254363 (pbk. ; alk. paper) | ISBN
   0814254365 (pbk. ; alk. paper)

Classification: LCC PS3568.O769 E95 2017 | DDC 811/.54—dc23

LC record available at https://lccn.loc.gov/2017026629

Cover photo and design by Michael J. Rosen

Text design by Juliet Williams

Type set in Janson Text

9 8 7 6 5 4 3 2 1

Contents

On Longevity / 1

I. Laws of Nature

Fledglings / 5

A Knock Upon the Senses / 6

Totem / 8

White-Tailed Deer, Winter / 10

The Skies in Our Heads / 11

Blind / 12

Haiku, Winter / 13

GEORGICS

On Celebrations / 19

On Varmints / 20

On Blood / 22

On Still Reflections / 24

On the Invisible / 26

On Making a Difference / 27

On Black Raspberries / 30

On Spinning / 32

On Brooding / 34

On Japanese Beetles / 35

On Apples / 37

On Poison Ivy / 39

On Soybeans / 40

On Firewood / 41

On Tree Sounds / 42

On Living Fences / 44

On Snow / 46

On Subdivisions / 47

On Your Nature / 49

On Grass / 51

On Shooting Stars / 53

On a Redwood / 56

Haiku, Spring / 59

II. Laws Other Than Nature's

Haiku, Summer / 65

At Present / 68

A Friend Phones to Say My Footprints Have Melted / 70

For the ever-optimistic / 72

Morel Season / 73

Passers-by / 75

Memory, Like Ice / 77

On Hearing That, 2,000 Miles Away, Your Friend's Dog Has Just Run Off / 79

Sighting / 82

Haiku, Autumn / 83

Once Upon a Trail / 87

On Longevity

Like the mayfly's single day of life,
or even the weeks granted butterflies—
their wings light as eyelids blinking—

consider even the decade or more that graces
the wild creatures you shelter beneath your roof:
Every species of hope, at least when held

within your grasping hands, appears too brief.
The future, by its very nature, isn't long
for this world.

Laws of Nature

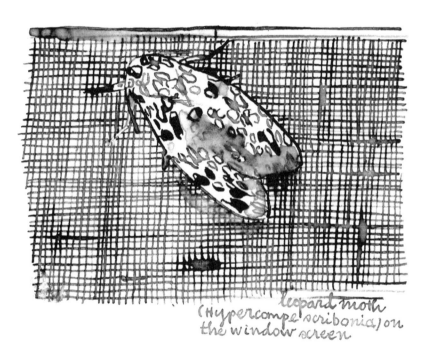

leopard moth
(Hypercompe scribonia) on
the window screen

Fledglings

*One of the baby robins jumped from its nest! And it can't fly yet.
And there's a mean old cat on our block. I put on garden gloves, ran
through two yards, jumped over fences, and finally returned it to the
nest. I felt so responsible. I was trying to snap a photo, and it jumped.*

—from a friend's letter

But that's what fledging is.
What's next is always a leap.
Each has to scramble and hide
a few days after it's fallen,
learning to forage for grubs
and bugs and berries, stretching

its wings, literally,
and building the strength to rise
into the air, to rise
against the odds—that cat,
for one. That's how the earth
feeds more than robins.

You and your camera,
you could have been a snake,
a crow, a common grackle,
a blue jay, a squirrel,
a raccoon, a sudden gust
or clatter, the thwack of a branch—

life is simply startling.
It's never just winging it
from the edge of now
into a safety net.
Next is always a leap,
not only for fledglings.

A Knock Upon the Senses

One too-early dusk while you were abroad,
     I heard a knocking, but oddly, not at the door
it seemed, and not on glass and not the limbs
     rattling against the eaves (there was no breeze),
but the inquiring rap of a visitor

that even the dogs' frantic barking confirmed.
     Yet one by one the doors revealed no guest,
nothing blurred from movement in the dark
     where we have only lately moved, where,
to judge from the specious proximity of lights

alone, the stars are now our closest neighbors.
     The tapping returned, even before I'd found
my place in the dropped book: distinct beats,
     five in a row—what knuckles would rap announcing
arrival, but muffled, as if the hand were gloved.

It would be untrue not to mention fear
     had played its usual part as I rushed
among our doors hoping to find a prankster
     heading for the pines, some urchin leaving
something unwanted or wanting something

luck hasn't provided. But with the next patter,
     I witnessed "the intruder," if that's what living
here invites: beside the bedroom feeder,
     a Carolina chickadee, head down,
hammering at insects in the cedar wall.

Of course, my standing there answered its call
        and made it flee as though it were unwelcome.
It will be back before you're home, and all
        you will have missed is a glimpse of me at the glass,
rattled at the apparent sound of alone.

Totem

All but a trunk the size of, say, a man
holding another man upon his shoulders
(the second's legs straddling his neck),
lies attenuated beside the elm,

its bark a paler shade that fails to lengthen
with our own days. Sheered by a gale
or hewn by lightning, or simply felled
by age or blight or rot, the headless sentry,

which must have overseen a century
of strange succession, now bears a crown
of splinters above a pocked, ungodly face
that woodpeckers forged with their incessancy.

Below, like gnarled wings or broken beaks,
fire brackets, belted polypores,
and flanks of Dryad's saddle mushroom
vivisected to the bark that's flayed

in segments to reveal the sinewy muscle
and civilizations of insects in between.
Where branches used to flex their bony elbows
now vacant sockets glare in each direction:

some with blockages of ancient nests,
one compounded with the bee's chthonian hum,
another that squirrels have all but packed with nuts,
and one that's ample enough for a possum's brood.

At its feet, among the roots whose grip
gravity has pried from earth, chipmunks
or moles or critters a dog can smell reside,
invisible to all but the barred owl

(itself invisible save a jeering, staccato
question that, like a spirit voice, is here
and everywhere, preoccupying the night;
I've yet to bring it closer with an answer).

Each winter day, when even the living
trees are naked skeletons awaiting
a resurrection, you cannot miss this totem,
singled out from all its lofty peers.

Come spring, it's easier to miss—
or dozens of other trees whose fates are carved
similarly, trees, which for this life
I share with another man, are ours,

ours by law, a law other than nature's.
But still I hope (and here I could be wrong,
if hope is simply the will to live at odds
with fearfulness, even your fear that faith,

whatever you've found of it, will not suffice
at last), that these guardians maintain
their vigil even if we propitiators
can only offer a vow: never to add

the chainsaw's grimace to their countenance.

White-Tailed Deer, Winter

deer tracks cross the ice
nothing but hunger to read
within their hooves' quotes

single-file deer path
now . . . our steps retrace theirs . . . now
their steps retrace ours

among plowed cornstalks
deer freeze, a stand of scarecrows,
scared of where we stand

unrelenting snow
buries all but the ivy
deer manage to eat

still as a statue
six-point buck stands in the yard
its nature: cement

buck hooves' half hearts—iced
into the fossil record
of February

The Skies in Our Heads

In gray and heavy cloaks, skulking clouds
cycle overhead; they kidnap color.

But even bleaker than snow or thunderstorms,
is all they forecast: gloom, unmoving gloom.
They're a sullen lot, a sit-in opposed
to optimism's slightest bright spot.

No matter. The sky's brooding—its threat
to hold its breath and *never* turn blue . . .

it never lasts. Sunlight's lances oust
the clouds, moodiness passes, and brilliance
hoists the dampened spirits of all the colors
that, moments ago, were hidden in plain sight.

These same relentless clouds
cycle in our heads, no different than sky.

Blind

Christmas morning, in pouring rain, we trail
the three charges of our hearts' domain as the dogs,
in turn, pursue invisible trails of deer
across a forest floor that's oddly free
of shotgun shells considering the fusillade
that has besieged the forest walls and fields,
sunup to sunset, this hunting season.

Volleyed cans of beer. The treads of trucks.
And sure enough, at the property's nearest edge,
within sight of the house: A crude teepee
of stalks encircles a trunk, another blind
brazenly erected without permission
(not that we'd have given it and not
that deer were safer for our withholding).

The dogs hasten ahead to what's left of the screen:
shattered as a window pane, it frames a view
of the glistening, deserted road—it *is* Christmas—
and the dormant, unsheltering fields beyond.
Our eyes were fooled. Closer, we see that lightning
erected—*wrecked*, rather, this hunter's blind,
snapping a maple's canopy and gutting

the heartwood in splinters the very width
and ochre of cornstalks: A scattershot
of spears discharged in every direction. Finally,
wet enough, we withdraw, slogging homeward
beneath a heaven that continues to threaten,
each of us game, each of us part of the season.

Haiku, Winter

white-tail deer shed,
dried seed pods of irises

single file, grackles
pace the thawing fields of snow
among sheered cornstalks

across the meadow,
everywhere is melted snow
save my boots' iced steps

old snow, it takes you
to remind me how many
travel this same way

heading out, I find
cat tracks, frozen in last night's
boot tracks, heading in

backlit by snow clouds
even scarlet cardinals
are gray silhouettes

now the snow falling
is fallen snow the trees held
as long as they could

inches of new snow . . .
among the tree shadows' warp,
the weaving dog's woof

watercress ripples
in the thawing stream's mouth: one
oasis from ice

amid stubs of stalks
in the snow-packed cornfield, blue
floats in one ice cloud

GEORGICS

What makes the cornfield smile; beneath what star
Maecenas, it is meet to turn the sod
Or marry elm with vine; how tend the steer;
What pains for cattle-keeping, or what proof
Of patient trial serves for thrifty bees;
Such are my themes.
—Virgil, *Georgics*

squirrel corn
(Dicentra
canadensis)

On Celebrations

See it there? Among the sodden leaves
that yet withhold their final gasps of crimson,

ocher, and orange-yellow as autumn exhales
every last green, something reflects

the dim daylight of an overcast dawn:
a cipher, a porthole in the forest floor,

or—oh: a helium balloon.
The bold and bleached letters herald, "HAPPY—"

Happy what? Whatever the wish was
faded as if to remind whoever stumbles

upon such a scrap that happiness
always drifts from its hopeful, deliberate course—

gravity, alone, is not to blame—
and then deflates, littering what lies ahead.

Squeeze out the last bites of breath
it holds. Brush off the bits of leaf and soil.

Tuck the lost pronouncement in your pocket
like a handkerchief. Pitch it in the trash

when you get home. Please, don't forget:
You do not want to find it there, hours

or even seasons later, a keepsake of—
the occasion escapes you. What's to celebrate

is a day in fall you found this weathered remnant.

On Varmints

Disremember *adorable*, which only
bespeaks of your own youth and ignorance.
The raccoons' bandit mask and crafty hands—
that infant face carried into adulthood!—

these are tactical measures, a strategy to scrounge
grubs beneath the sod (the barely living
sod you've ransomed all season from the fields).
Live and let live? Which one? The grass?

All you welcome will be held against you:
The Scales of Justice are clearly night-blind.
The very animals whose telltale presence
had modeled your vision of country life, shaped it

as Pygmalion had his own ideal, these
will be the creatures you curse beneath your breath,
defend to locals who volunteer to shoot
whatever fits the nomenclature *varmint*.

But how can wilderness observe your codes?
That bees should pollinate your plantings but not
mistake the lawn you mow for nesting ground;
that snakes should filch their share of mice yet never

reveal their cold, infernal selves to you.
If deer could only be a hologram,
a visible idea of deer to offer
metaphors of grace and innocence,

and not the living flesh that shears your saplings,
that rots along the gravel shoulder where a car
(not yours, this time) had swerved, that multiplies
within the acres your own kind has claimed.

Must you define the nature that you love
by virtue of your absence from it? Must it exist
like the old country you've left or only knew
from family anecdotes you tired of hearing

and now cannot, for the life of you, recall?

a tattered regal moth —
(citheroni regalis)
the hickory horned devil —
fluttering and dragging across
the meadow

On Blood

Try: You might find consolation
    by citing "law of nature,"
an obligatory course
    of study you'd undertaken in your youth
and merely forgotten like so many
    foreign tongues you longed to master.

Likewise, you may be inclined
    to see this mole, the cat's first catch
(first, that is, you chanced to see),
    as beneficial, considering
the minions whose tunnels monogrammed
    your lawn in scorched, browning loops.

Yet this baby robin splayed
    upon the welcome mat, maimed
but not yet dead, is harder to dismiss:
    Both cat and bird are fledglings
in their different elements,
    as you are when it comes to blood.

Friends will urge you to see these victims
    as tributes the cat is offering you.
Try that as well. Think all you like
    about the eggs pilfered from nests,
nests flung from swaying boughs,
    hatchlings swallowed by snakes, starved

by siblings, snatched in flight by hawks—
        causes you deem natural, beyond
the confines of your yard and conscience.
        But this one that your housecat wounds,
that she delivers into your field
        of vision, must this one be your charge,

sanctioned within your heart just like
        its killer, the once-stray cat?
You wrap the bird in a paper bag
        and end its suffering (not yours)
with the stomp of your heel—which summons the cat,
        and, instantly, your anger rises

as you lunge toward this beast you shelter,
        allow to curl against your shoulder
at night as if she were your dreams'
        familiar, and yet, you understand,
the moment you seize the scruff of her neck,
        you have no lesson to teach. Or learn.

Is it harder knowing there's nothing
        you can do, or that this death
is nothing, nothing more or less
        than your own cat's blank stare:
green with a core of darkness
        where you, too, must be reflected.

On Still Reflections

Against the hillock of volunteer
sugar maples and red elms
from which a bullying wind is trying
to shake the last of summer, against
the covenanted green of pines
(twenty thousand the late owners
had planted thirty years ago
on an overgrazed farmstead)—

you sight a flash of white and blue:
A kingfisher (confirmed in your guide)
splashes to the gold-leafed water,
dips, nabs, or misses something,
and ascends to an opposite branch
in the arc of an aerialist
that leaves you gazing toward the vaster
kingdom of white and blue above.

Downward, skyward, now it's filched
some innocent—pray, what?—in its beak.
The bird continues to entertain—
no, *eat*—dazzling you
at the mammoth picture window that prizes
the scene like a memento—*prevents*
the likes of you from being seen.
Selection—nature's or not—is art.

The next and the next day, it returns,
but never when you have a witness
with whom to share it, never before
its rattling call rouses you
and its plunge has shattered the inverted
trees mirrored there, erasing,
for a moment, that perfect division
between the reflected and the real.

Later, shuffling through radiant leaves
along the shoreline, you reconsider:
Does the pond need dredged, its banks
reshaped, as the county agent advised?
Must the pines be thinned as planned?
What would, say, thirty years of natural
succession afford you, the present owner,
subject of the same prevailing winds?

What will make the kingfisher stay
besides your own leave-taking?

belted
kingfisher
on a lichen-covered branch

On the Invisible

Dew-soaked, the dog's
paws watermark
the tiles, each print more dim,

as if his steps were fading
from memory, not sight . . .
like a gift or a note

of sympathy you've meant
to send that's been foregone
and, finally, forgotten . . .

until you reach the kitchen,
the jar of treats, and then,
there's just no sign of him.

On Making a Difference

For weeks, the cardinal darts among the barbed
leaves of the holly, then undulates to the wire—
chit, chit—where she perches until you go.
You gather she's woven a nest but only see it
the night your cat
                        flings itself into the bush,
toppling a coarse twining of needles and twigs.
You scream at the cat,
                        toss a plastic pot
to startle her—you'd been kneeling, planting—
and stand too fast, *your knees* almost buckling.
You race, light-headed, across the lawn
and reach your gloved, ungainly hands
to lift two things that look no more like birds
than human embryos, their closed eyes—
a bulge of darker pink on paler pink—
sightless as the aureoles on your breast.
Their beaks gape, round and impossibly wide,
as you attempt to orient them, fragile
within the fragile nest you wedge higher
inside the holly, lacerating your skin
as you brace it with limbs the cat's
                                    leap snapped.
You step away, hoping the hatchlings can signal
the *mother* and *father* (that's not sentimental)
who watch—*chit . . . chit*—from a distance,
as does the cat.
            Get! Get the hell out—
You have to believe the parents will hear them rustle.
(You sense their maws can do no more than swallow.)
You have to believe the cat,
                        suddenly, won't hear.

From *now on, the cat*

          stays indoors!—

The thought passes, as do the songs of birds,
as do the images of other nests . . .
seasons—acres of nests you never saw,
although the cat

         may have, and you, you
could never have saved them all. It's hard to say
if you've saved this one. It's worse, isn't it,
that it's *your* cat

         and not an owl or snake
that has—that will have—nothing to do with you?
Chit. Chit. The male and female call . . .
only to each other? Have they abandoned
the hatchlings now that the cat

            has found them?
—or now that you have? And then you reason,
the cat

        could have killed them instantly—
and would have, had you not intervened.
Now it's death by shock, starvation, cold,
which must be worse than death by predator.
You have no hand to hold the hand of fate.
Finally, the female descends to a holly bough
and disappears among the leaves. *Chit* . . .
Your eyes follow the leaves that shift with her hops,
imagining the story you cannot see.
She's nowhere near where you've replaced the nest.
Chit . . . the seconds between each call . . . *chit* . . .
increase. And then she flies out, perching
along the wire from where her mate has called,
nonstop. From what you think is a safe
distance, you watch until there's only darkness

to watch. The parents, the hatchlings, you—all
but your cat,

        the cat

           you took in
. . . how many years ago? dazed and starving
behind the house in the middle of the nowhere
you live—all but the cat

              give up.

Slinky, one of the resident
cats, patiently waiting at the door

On Black Raspberries

You come to expect the serpent-like
poison ivy besieging each fruit
and path of this blessed place
two have purchased with a single future.

You come to know the thorns as well,
incising blood lines fainter
than the inescapable juice
that murderously stains the flesh.

You came prepared—however pointless—
with citronella spray, your ears
already droning with mosquitoes,
your neck pricked by deer flies.

But these—they come as pure surprise.
Around the meadow's edge, wherever
the violet-black berries are heaviest,
a daddy longlegs—dozens

within a brandished thicket of berries—
suckles juice from one lobe
of a raspberry cap, scrambles down
the bramble at your fingers' approach.

Even from childhood you counted
these frail, stilt-gaited beings
among the world's few harmless things,
but whether they panic as they flee,

fear harm from you—or anything else—
you cannot guess, though, like a fear,
that unknowing is now attached,
spider-like itself, to the berries,

as you reach across the ivy
and among the protection of thorns,
swatting with the left hand, choosing
—always for our kind—with the right.

chanterelles

On Spinning

A lifeline trails each move
a spider makes, weaving mullions from which
it spies the universe.

Imagine if humans, too,
could see the rambling course we've roamed in search
of sustenance and love.

What if, like arachnids, we could retrace
the tenuous lines we've left,
repair or even consume that past, and twist it

into another future?
(As for what we spin, hope may be
our closest homologue.)

Yet nothing we make, nothing on Earth, can match
the spider's strands for strength.
Already men and women of science are tasked

with harnessing the spider's
skill for uses once thought wild but now
fall well within the powers

of imagination: a silk for bulletproofing
clothes, for hulls of jets,
for patching valves inside a failing heart.

This question is not
unlike the one Arachne must have considered,
pitting the art of her loom

against Athena, oblivious to triumph's
aftermath, to what
is left a soul that humbles gods. Arachne

hanged herself in the forest,
and to this day, each path you clear still bears
witness to her handiwork,

invisible as guilt or fear or any
consequence of choice
until a web snaps across your face

and you lurch backwards, plucking
the gauze that clings with shells and legs and wings
of other victims to your skin.

So far, the spiders will not cooperate:
In any factory
that's built for them, the brutes devour each other

before they can submit
to the diabolic labor of another race.
Now we must ask ourselves,

will anything escape the force of nature
that is our joined, ungodly
desire? Remember: We answer once and for all.

On Brooding

Beneath the peak of the barn's eaves,
bald-faced hornets fabricate
their nest: each week, a larger and larger
teardrop as if holding back
more and still more grief. The gray
of recycled news, it mocks the barn—
it may well *be* the barn, its rotting timbers
gnawed, chewed, and spit-glued in pages
thin as wishes, wrapping the new brood.
Or maybe their nest is younger trees,
elms succeeding the native oaks
in the century since the barn's raising . . .
since you began your own yearly repairs.
With the first frost, their story breaks.

jack-in-the-
pulpits flower
in the shade
near a spring

On Japanese Beetles

Abstractly, the concept of sharing persuades.
You divvy up a garden into yours
and all the rest beyond your control.

Cherries above the ladder's reach belong
to birds; likewise, you forfeit those closest
to the ground, which untold deer will claim.

The deer's take you offset with the beasts'
beauty, with vague atonement for a race
with longer memory of this land than you.

The birds, too, are redeemed within our eyes
and ears, and for the meals they make of what
we nominate as pests. But nature's never

asked that we, of all creation, weigh
each species in its balance; mercifully,
no other has assessed our own.

But what of creatures we cannot justify?
Mornings, armed with a bucket of water and soap,
you comb the rose beds, plucking what seems to be

the sunlight's glint upon the leaves (if only
it were something so beneficent or brief),
but is, instead, *Popillia japonica*—

invader-turned-native a century ago—
buried in the burst heart of a rare blossom
or flensing a leaf to its venous skeleton.

Hard as it is, you must train yourself,
just as you have trained each hybrid rose
and still forbear its yearly disappointments

(black spot, mildew, winter kill),
that every drowning is not a victory,
either for roses or for humankind.

The next morning, the bucket's a putrid slurry,
while bushes radiate with pestilence
as though your intervention were nothing but

a forbidding cloud in a sun-bright sky.
How many mornings, roses, deaths, defeats
until you can resign yourself to choice:

Uproot the roses and tend your dream of perfection—
continual blooms in every fragrance and hue—
or keep the roses and, like the beetles, return

each summer to your godforsaken lot.

Japanese beetles
(Popillia japonica)
perforating a maple leaf

On Apples

How much of the world you know by heart
is unidentified, subsumed under
the Order Weed or Bird or Insect/Bug?
How many trees are nothing beyond "the woods"?

How odd, then, suddenly to find apples
underfoot—gnarled, pocked, greenish fruits—
below a towering, half-dead tree you've passed
a thousand times in the seasons you've shared this land.

Tuned, now, to the cloying scent of cider,
you notice the same bark, the same branching
on half a dozen nearby trunks, each one
familiar and untended as the first.

What was this landscape like when all these trees
were saplings, when generations ago someone
dreamed of an orchard—but why so far from a house,
by elms and maples that all but own the sun?

Later, it dawns on you that no one but deer
have planted the apple trees, just as birds
have sown the bramble of blackberries, black
raspberries, and dogwoods that ring your fields.

So now, after fifty or eighty years
of tortured, shaded, ivy-strangled growth,
it's apples of your very own you desire, hanging
so high in the canopy that even the lowest

are beyond a ladder or any deer's leap.
You watch them swell and blush, blemish and skew,
you even entertain the notion of rigging
some scaffold or inveigling the fire fighters . . . .

But summer beats on, and the unripe fruits drop,
which was always their course before your paths:
no one eating the apples, no one noting
their fall. But now with you as witness and heir,

it's suddenly a crime to let the apples rot,
spoiling like the berries too far within
the brambles, entwined among the poison ivy.
How is it that merely because the trees' lives

have reached into your own passage, you,
like Tantalus, are tormented by what's beyond
your grasp? Let the flesh, like the seeds, return
to earth. Absolve yourself this once, from the taking.

On Poison Ivy

Of uselessness, nature will not condone
a single instance: Serve or fail to survive.

So how, in all of evolution, did one
innocuous ivy require a venom to thrive,

an essence so virile that, tender or dried,
root or leaf—or even the cloud of its burning—

the slightest contact causes the flesh to erupt?
And since this plant will harm no other hide

in the Animal Kingdom, when did our kind
vie for its light or space, threaten the vine's

dominion, which must, by now, be nearly secured?
We would have spared it—would have spared ourselves

the hapless warfare of sprays and blades, the weeks
prying loose its gratuitous, gloating hold

on any path we clear across the wild.
But now it is too late to retreat. The poison

is all that has not fled the garden in fear.
We must accept the ivy as if it were

temptation. Ingest it, bit by bit, and from
its vengeance, savor a brief immunity.

On Soybeans

Overnight, the soybean meadows
    convert to gold
as though a god, indeed, had descended
    as a shower of coins,
transforming the green to something more
    immortal than cash.
Winds rustle the radiant tillage:
    a gloating miser
whose fingers dredge and seine the hoarded,
    plundered spoils.
Suddenly, the acres are worth their weight
    in gold—at least,
their sowers' hopes are. But metamor-
    phoses continue:
The coins drop, the stalks rattle
    their dried pods,
and, in the offing, the droning harvesters
    level the field.
There are no gods or misers here.
    We all inherit
chaff. The only alchemy
    is turning yourself
toward and not away from it.

On Firewood

The ice storm cleaves
        the century-
old oak,
      and in an instant
fifty years
        lay siege
to your whole yard,
     barring passage
as if they sensed
     how you'd turn back
given the chance.
      At first light,
the saws descend,
      wailing over
the loss, splitting
    the dense limbs
in bearable rounds.
     The log splitter
halves and halves
      until the rings
are hewn in quarters
     and reassembled
in a barricade
    as long as the fence
but even higher,
     demonstrating
how little room
    you have to grow.
Eventually
you won't see
the missing half
beside the fifty
years that stand.
In the fireplace
the cured wood
lasts but minutes.

On Tree Sounds

Out of doors,
borrowing the deer's
tapered paths among the jewelweed, trillium, cutleaf toothwort
(wildflowers that were
invisible until you met them here),
the quiet is so familiar

you wonder where
the creatures are
who share
the forest floor
—corn snake, squirrel, eastern salamander—
how is it, day after day, it's rare

to even sense their presence; odder
still to think that you, too, may be no more
than a rare
sight in the understory.
But then, curiously, still nowhere
near a door of any sort,

you hear
that familiar
groaning of a door on its hinge, a door
—admittedly, an enormous door—
opening in the otherwise silent air
as if someone were trying to dress or

undress or
pack and not wake you before
the precautious alarm reports
it's already later:
You're face to face with another
day and, soon enough, the day after.

You stare
at the canopy, scanning the limbs, the inter-
leaving patches of light—off-white, mauve, azure—
as if that creaking might recur,
but like a flitting, elusive singer
that's veiled by foliage so that no wing bar,

ruddy breast, or eye ring will let you declare
you've never seen its kind before,
adding another to the life list (chances are
you have seen it), the sound refuses an encore.
The limb, the trunk, the wood that might have been a door
remains shut, or

maybe open, held ajar
by nothing but a gesture,
a hand, a hope that's both as clear
and as clearly obscured
as that skyward portal or
the fellow creatures

who claim these selfsame acres
in which we plant our years.
We're all mortal
seeds—meadowsweet, goldenseal, squirrel corn—
each a mere
fortune, each a miraculous volunteer.

On Living Fences

The deer wend their way amid the woods,
plotting a narrow, single-file path
among brambles, blockading trees, barbs
of wire, blackberry, and wild rose.

You take their lead, placing your inarticulate
feet over the quotes their hooves have printed:
paired half-moons some other, earlier nation
had scrawled to tell its travels to the future.

With chainsaw, mower, and leather gloves you clear
a wider swath, so you can walk erect
and without ducking, without mangling yourself
among the rampant multiflora roses

that are no more native to this place than you,
a virulent hybrid merchandized to farmers
seventy years ago as living fences,
feckless spires of predacious thorns

to keep the deer from the crops, the livestock from harm.
But now they do not border your fallow acres;
they are one and the same: Within/without,
wanted/unwanted . . . the difference is lost—or won.

Mornings as you trace these paths you've added
to your maintenance list, you place your waffled soles
among the deer's notations: Fear; the pheromones
of the dogs that always accompany you

as if they served more than your childlessness;
the practice rounds, year-round, of neighbors' guns—
these haven't changed their common story a jot.
Perhaps they know no other ending; hapless

as this sounds to you, some season far,
or not so far, from now (not that deer
can sense the difference), you could find yourself
following their worn and silent example.

When there is nowhere to escape
all the paths will lead there.

cornotalk stubble in snow

45

On Snow

Snow is a covenant you make
with winter. Like love or faith, it renews itself
each day—not always as predicted.
Today your road's impassable . . . tomorrow

the sun appears as if to apologize . . .
sheets of ice careen from the eaves . . .
then freezing rain . . . and then, who knows, snow
that's perfect for packing, as if, inside you still,

there is a morning, knee-deep in drifts,
a fort of enormous snowballs that outlasts
bitter winds and thaws of sudden warmth,
to wash up, blunted as beach glass,

across the sodden green of early March.
Beneath the snow, winter's hard-packed
with such sharp remembered shards. Seasons
bury emotion: a tilth that crumbles in your hand.

On Subdivisions

Whatever idyllic pretense, lust for the past,
or pastoral ideal beckoned you
to this hinterland, no matter the acres
of forest, flood plains, tillable fields,

or untamed meadows that shield this haven you've pledged
your life to keep, hold forever in mind
that you are merely the latest claim in a history
of impositions, all of them too late.

Just as the veins of minerals that course beneath
your hallowed lawn and gardens are leased to others,
just as the icy aquifer withholds
its every insinuation, so, too, the dreams

you have for this, your home, are not your own.
Among the season's changing hues (hidden
even as brown and red await within the first
unfurling green of the leaf) will be the pink

of the surveyor's ribbons, the white signs
of realtors that parse the rage of wildflowers
into a dozen identical square-foot lots
and raze the woods as though their verticals

obstructed the greater horizontal good.
Your vast and precious view will then be sectioned,
scarred with asphalt, sutured with power lines.
As with erosion, this cannot be reversed:

Each year, the mountains forfeit inches from
their summits; oceans will never be as deep.
Stockpile your hopes for this, your refuge,
and they will wear away until there's nothing

but more, and then more of you to see.
The longer you stay, the more unbearable
the loss, yet even this you must part with:
Forgive your neighbors as you have yourself.

metal mark
maybe tawny
emperor?

On Your Nature

Why are we tempted (and why do I ally
myself with "we" when I can only mean
myself with certainty . . . while certainty,
above all, is a thing to doubt)—why
is it we look for signs in the expression
of a season's early or late or thwarted heralds,
where the natural, bridled with human longing,
becomes not "un-" but "preternatural": a world

of difference. The cavalcade of crabapples
that shrouds the road to the vet's with its rash
pink (a shade approaching the skin's embarrassment)
will bear for us, in perpetuity,
as if it were the blooms' perfume, the weight
of our first retriever on the day we put him down.
The trees, the arborists, the neighbors we pass—none
acknowledge this, none can mock or console.

Let's say, the week before a relative dies,
when every telephone call could be the news,
the gravel drive is dotted with stone-still skippers,
metalmarks, monarchs, a sky's worth
of blues: the blue copper? the common blue?—
more butterflies than you can ever recall.
The road provides them no shelter, food, or drink.
Some wait on the steps, but not to accompany you.

Why or how have they gathered here, you wonder,
with no "as though," "as if," or "like" in mind:
their powdery wings held high and flush together
with no homologous sense of prayer, of hands
that close some wanting between their stalled gestures.
Their upright wings confess taxonomy,
that's all: They differ from the legions of moths
whose wings lie flat, beside or across their backs.

You need not classify each one; knowing
depletes as often as it completes a life.
It only matters that, from this day forward,
even if you learn that Lepidoptera
cannot fly when their bodies drop below
a temperature of eighty-six and they must bask
in a sun-warmed place to gain the use of wings,
you sense that butterflies are only the beginning.

Soon, you must conscript the whole of nature,
assigning, one by one, its every piece
to your most certain insignificance.

On Grass

Every blade of grass has its angel that bends
over it and whispers, "Grow, grow."
—Talmud

You cannot hear the chorus of the lawn,
the infinitude of angels urging each
lowly, trodden blade to lift its head.
For them, as for all creation, heaven is what
exists beyond a reach.

You need not hear their words in order to listen.

If such devotion attends the common grass,
imagine what must resound from higher up
within the evergreens' exalted boughs,
among the thriving trees, abundant with nuts
or weeping with fruit that even

the angels desire, although they have no hunger.

Consider, then, the woods' sublime refrain,
with choristers who murmur at every birth
or breath of any species who dwells within.
The power of that one repeating word,
that fervent, patient drone,

must rival the wind, though it is stillness.

And as for you, how often has that word
been chanted above your head as each cell
divided, determining its two new selves?
Is there a horde of emissaries attending
your wild fecundity,

the untold substitutions that preserve you

as you: the immoderate hairs and irrelevant nails,
the skin that thickens or scars, bruises or sheds,
the seeds of life your body sacrifices
as though in blind obedience to some god
whose ways you comprehend

only by the testimonies of mortals?

Just as you might speak to the unborn
or to a loved one fading past all care
and any earthly reassurance you bear,
it is not the wisdom of your words but the will
to utter them that matters.

Likewise, these chanted words are nothing but will.

On Shooting Stars

The Leonid meteor shower, in November of 2001,
was predicted to be the most resplendent display of
lights in its 33.2-year cycle around the sun.

Set the bedside clock to rouse you
even amid your deepest dreams:
This year's the rarest chance to witness
this comet dust we've misnamed stars.

Keep the house as dark as the night.

Bundle in your bathrobe and boots
and shuffle across the damp lawn.
Search amid the firmament
for a streak, a trail as faint as a scratch

within a sepia print of some prim
and dashing relation you know is yours
although no one alive—you
least of all—can claim to have met.

Head out farther into the pitch.

Cloud cover, the canopy of pines,
the neighbor's vapor light—something
obscures the shower. Drive the car
until it's dark enough to see.

Switch off the headlights. You'll find yourself

in blackness as dense as the middle of a woods.
It takes a moment for the eyes to adjust,
a moment for this to seem natural:
a human stalled in the darkness without

a clear desire to make for the light.

Amid your sky's quotidian stars,
(mysterious despite their fixity)
new lights have journeyed here—
albeit three hundred years before you—

just as you have. Count them:

twelve . . . forty . . . you've never seen
but two such stars in all your years.
At ninety-nine you leave off counting,
as if suddenly your wealth

were such that you could want for nothing
another star might yet provide.
What is to say these dim, diminished
bodies do not likewise count you

among their short-lived marvels?

Back home, in bed, it hardly matters
if you close your eyes or keep them open:
Stars persist. A red beacon
awaits a message from anywhere.

A constellation keeps watch
atop the nightstand's accumulations.
A blinking pinpoint signals
your earthly realm has been secured.

Sleep all you can. Come morning,

as with your dreams, you'll have nothing
to show for where you've been—your boots
will have dried, and light, flooded the house,
revealing your name on everything

and the world revolving around you again.

On a Redwood

One day, when your friend delivers
the pot-bound seedling,
the redwood bought in college,
shipped across the country,

and shuttled from porch to porch—
spindly needles dropping
like second hands our clocks
have all but given up—

plant it among your acres,
imagining the day
when it has grown the height
of thirty men and shaded

thirty generations.
Of all the evidence remaining
of how you lived to make
the world more peaceable

or just, consider this tree,
one infinitesimal part
on an Earth that could, by then,
be flooded, abandoned, or cold.

So much of what we do
will last a season: Our deeds
are annuals we choose
to sow again or not.

So much of what we pledge
extends for several years,
no more, as if the heart,
as well, rotates its yields.

So much of what we dream
bridges a generation,
the thirty years or so,
before the child has heirs.

So much of what we fear
looks toward the century,
the dimming likelihood
that we will see such change.

Time's rewards exceed
our chance ever to accept them.
You must consider now
for all eternity.

Haiku, Spring

birds nest
and pond
snail shells

spring—a wren shuttles
pine needles past my window,
tacking hope in place

spring must be closer—
rhododendron leaves uncurl
and light dims inside

rain all day, no choice
but to walk—my umbrella
soaking dog's left half

spring-green sweetgum leaf
already burnt orange and rust
lie in wait for fall

no, eyes! two spring weeks
and you may not overlook
a single green shock

such swift flowering—
spring beauties, you leave no space
to plant my footsteps

the parallel swells
of eight paddling mallards rule
the still lake's blank page

they're anonymous
these raindrops—and then, the stream
gives each one its name

last fall's lone pennant,
why are you still waving, leaf,
from spring's thawing bough?

fifty weeks of thorns
then, as if all's forgiven
the wild roses' scent

not even three weeks
the Bradford pear's wind-sheared stump
still insists on spring

run-off clouds the stream . . .
banks resume their age-old clash—
lost makes way for found

Laws Other Than Nature's

painted or box
turtle eggs from
the bank of the
farm pond, cardinal skull, dried spore "frond"
from ostrich ferns around the koi pond

Haiku, Summer

multiflora roses

morning cardinals
calling—does it wake me or
do I wake to it?

more rain this morning,
now even the scent of rain
has been rinsed away

already finches
and the just refilled feeder
still swings from my grasp!

one arched beech limb scrawls
its urgent ripples across
a dawdling current

half stinging nettles
and half Christmas ferns—how not
to think of life's path

If you'd never heard
the crows' caw-caw, would it be
unmistakable?

August's hot breezes
the halves of ourselves flip-flopped
along the clotheslines

a crescent moon's smile
the pond reflects as a frown:
night's parenthesis

no sunlight pierces
the forest's thatched roof—just shrieks
of one red-tailed hawk

an ancient tree falls
only our way is blocked—there
where more trees will fall

as if on command
the very thing I bring you
to see—there! it flees

At Present

You can't ride two horses with one rear end.

—Yiddish proverb

Someday, it might be possible
to be two places at once.
Even if the science is lacking,
maundering behind the mind's addled
and antsy ravenousness, we first
must master one place
at one time. But it's not planting
both feet in the present saddle
that cues up the unmanageable;
it's that the rest of the self is AWOL:

The ears are off to eavesdrop.
The fingers betray an inner disquiet.
The tongue keyboards the teeth
in mute refrains of impatience.
The eyes' frantic kaleidoscope
entrances . . . far and near—*Focus!*
Here! No . . . over here!
And don't forget the periphery!—
to say nothing (and everything?)
of the persistent banter between
the neighboring hemispheres.

And so to be two places
at the same time, setting a foot
in one stirrup and then the other
on a second mount, compounds the feat.
"Forward, ho!" to one means
"Let's go back," to the other.
(And that presumes each knows who's leading.)
The single option, provisional
as it may seem, is standing ground:
span the choice between either and or
as if they were not one and the same.

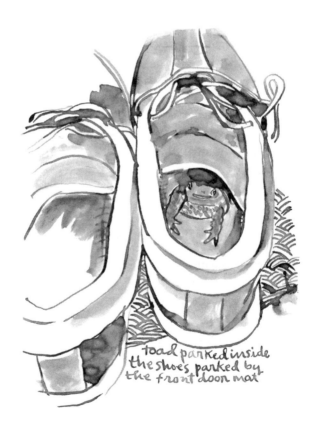

toad parked inside
the shoes parked by
the front door mat

A Friend Phones to Say My Footprints Have Melted

What we revere of snow's weightless
particles—besides that precious
individuality
we like to claim as kindred proof
of our own distinctive, ephemeral fates—
are its revelations in
this otherwise weighty world—
how, accumulated, it shows
what sight cannot: a shape for wind
as visible as wafting drapes,
the scurry of animals a dog
discerns without the snow's dusting,
our own unconscious thoroughfares
of use. Every falling, a surprise.

But once we put our hands on it,
once it's packed beneath our feet
and flakes conform to frozen designs—
a shoe's tread, a wheel's furrow,
the keys fumbled at the frozen lock—
snow retells like poetry:
the mold of a lingering moment
compacted into another present
and revealed, if at all, only
once the weight of happenstance
lifts and rolls onto the next
impressionable expanse of white.
Every footprint in the snow,
for instance, recalls the same goodbye.

Yet even these articulations
of absence thaw and disappear,
just as each print required the foot's
departure in order to announce itself,
just as each line reprinted here
leaves its moot impression only
once your eyes abandon it.
Consider the ground, absorbing all,
never sensing in water's release
a difference between snow or tear.
Those footprints were to be forgotten
the very moment they were made.
Likewise, the goodbyes. Take this,
their frozen ellipsis, to heart.

the houndmix
Ticker's legs jumbled
as ever when asleep

For the ever-optimistic

cat, who *can't* be hungry, the marble altar
where salvation from a pitiless yearning may poise
is such a storied climb it might as well
be heaven where a prayer or wish's outcome
is always iffy, at least in terms of timing.
Patience is for the damned. It's purgatory.

He cannot see if there is fish or cheese
that might float down—even a mere morsel—
or if the clap and clatter of he who tends the hearth
foretells that any promise has been dashed,
sacrificed to the infernal disposal
that rocks and spatters . . . and roars with needless gloating.

No matter. Each meal, the cat attends
the rug beside my unpredictable feet.
"Trust me," I say to him on those numerous days
when he gazes upward as I cube tofu
or spoon some grapefruit marmalade on toast,
"Really, you don't want this." And yet he stays

as if to prove his devotion unwavering.
And so I place a tidbit of this "manna"
before his feet. He bows his head and snuffles.
Returning my gaze, now his one and only
expression cannot belie his disbelief:
This! This *is how you reward your faithful?*

He backs away, his pure heart betrayed,
swearing this will never again come to pass,
never, nope, not in a million years . . .
which happens to coincide with the length of a nap.
How else to suffer life's belittlements
than to wake each time with hope's appetite.

Morel Season

bright dappling puzzles
the forest floor, already
in pieces since fall

*

spring's first warm nights . . .
sweeping branch, my second hand,
loses track of time

*

worn trails through wild woods
then a new path's loose, dark soil
what else can love clear?

*

amid canopies
of may apple, our steps are
the understory

*

the year's first morel!
now pupils can recall not
where to look but how

*

thick strips of elm bark
ring a bare trunk: blond morels
half-bent as we are

*

old, brittle basket
searching for mushrooms again
to carry us back

⁂

are they here . . . or here?
we hunt with memory's frost
as the morning warms

⁂

side by side since dawn . . .
Here's one! . . . Found one . . . suddenly
we hear we're shouting

⁂

conceding untold
mushrooms, we leave . . . they raise up
like hands with answers

⁂

these loud, crisp, browned leaves—
last June's shade, fall's reds—will be
chance's rich humus

Passers-by

On cockeyed barns, hand-lettered in old-
style gothic, the word, A N T I Q U E S, reminds us

of the obvious—like SCENIC VISTA signs,
proclaiming what we passers-by will miss
by definition: a hilltop and its valley
(swatches of field or farm quilted together
with power lines) and then another hilltop

(the return-trip vista) and so on. Having stretched
our imaginations, we climb back in the car.

How surprisingly little one can find, summoned
to the beautiful. You slip a finger between
the interrupted pages—whether leaning
to glimpse, beneath the airplane wing, a city
strung with houses strung with Christmas lights,

or to stand at the backdoor acknowledging
a warbler, icicles, the orange of the skyline—

my words—"impossibly orange"—prepare
your eyes for the all-too-possible.
So, asking, "lie still another moment,"
shifts something: Your weight, secured on my chest,
is suddenly hard to bear. All this is

as barely perceptible as a gaze glazing to a stare.
So we drive, pointing to what we won't let escape

our two attentions. The one who names it beautiful
becomes the beautiful in its stead (cloying
as a child who, mile after mile, asks,
"Are we out of Ohio yet?" as though
"yes," might be the actual destination).

Since you could name each object before I point,
the unremarked, hurtling past our windows,

reminds us what to watch out for: the claim
we lay to this, now that, then one another.
Our love for the world has been anonymous;
for each other, how we can't attribute
anything, beautiful or otherwise, to having

caused it. Remind me that "to last"
means as long as we are passing by.

daddy long-legs
arachnid but not a spider
(2 eyes, no silk, no venom)

Memory, Like Ice

The day of the early thaw, warmth and sun
seemed as far away as any place
you needed to be, spinning your wheels on a street
that offered little beyond the precedent
of other anxious cars' sgraffito tracks.

The stands of pine and even deciduous trees
whose weary bent limbs were burdened for days
with a brave impasto (titanium white;
an amateur job, compared with how a real
painter would have captured the feel of snow)

began to rain in droplets—yet thicker than rain,
a constant drizzle from the canopies
that soaked my shoulders and cap, the dogs' coats,
and plunked into the top half-inch of snow
like our footfalls, but myriad, minute.

All around us the bark glistened, refinished
with the seeping snow as though the woods
were wet still from Creation. (What odd distrust
compels the mind to varnish a view with talk
of Eden? Seeing is not belief enough?)

It hurt my eyes to see the meadow's white
that neither sun nor steps had burnished, taut
as sheets in a guest bedroom where no one sleeps.
Down the ravine, the buried stream broke
into water-like song, a long-held note

that rippled the ice and tinted the virgin snow,
disclosing fissures in the crust. Colossal chunks
already jutted from shore, shards that only
could have fallen from heaven's shattered dome.
(Another failed attempt, I know, at leaving

well enough alone.) Over and over,
I wished for you—or a Polaroid at least.
(If only dogs could be sufficient witness.)
But with the thought of cameras, I knew the hope
of seeing this again or ever sharing

what I'd seen was melting faster than ice.
I followed the stream—one bank, the opposite,
across the property line and back . . . and forth,
pretending I could learn the scene by heart
or add a feckless self to the scene's effusion,

yet all the while, I thought, tomorrow—*today*,
that is—you still might come and photograph
the stream . . . a different stream, I know, but still,
a stark passage of planes and verticals,
flawless whites, majestic this's and that's.

But then, at the crest of the rise—overlooking
the ravine, the water, the pines a last time—
I saw that today, let alone tomorrow,
was already too late: The paths—the *past*
I'd made—had spoiled what I'd wished preserved.

(Maybe ecstasy requires a brief
half-life to peak desire for the next?)
Shortly, conditions might be right again;
my awkward, well-meant steps will be erased.
So for the time being, take my word:

The intersecting whites, the lines of ice,
the snow in any direction you might have stared,
fell nothing shy of—believe me—divine.

On Hearing That, 2,000 Miles Away,
Your Friend's Dog Has Just Run Off

Picture this: During a telephone call,
your friend on the other end breaks off mid-sentence—
Hold on, I have to grab the dog—and drops
the receiver to her desk whose color, a cream . . .
no, white, you can recall, though inexactly.

From your end, you hear the shouts at the door
that opens onto the garden you so admired:
that higher voice that entreats a puppy to come,
then frantic, then fainter shouts, outside now,
as you suppose she rushes from the room.
But then, even that false echo fades
as though her voice were giving out already,
giving up before the endless search
has even begun (for panic must have no end
in sight), before the pointlessness of calling,
calling anything back from the point
of harm. Picture yourself—your auditory self—
alone in the silence of that distant house,
the phone a listening post, the room a place
you scan in memories from your visit months ago,
rooting about for keys, some kind of lead:
a mantle of souvenirs from . . . ?; yes, the books;
the indigo pencil beside answering machine;
a mullioned door swung open like the arm
of a sundial onto the little brickwork deck

her father had helped reset (she'd written you this)
with all the pots of . . . pansies? snapdragons?
that the dog would lie against, sensing
how he completed a picture there—however
fleeting (as this moment of fear can prove)—
of something condign and ideal, how he aligned,
with the pure effortlessness of his watch,
that tiniest part of the world we call the world.

And just as the distance between your friend and her dog
increases, so the miles and minutes expand
as you wait. Hang up and free the line—for what?
Continue to hold? Monitor the emptiness
of that abandoned place and the palpable void
a lost dog will bring into that house,
depositing it smack in the center of the floor
like a slobbery bone that all must step around?
Imagine her starting the car, the open garage—

the clack of footsteps. Your friend's voice returns.
But the dog, the dog, the miserable dog has not.
Halfway down the block, your friend, she had to—
(imagine her midstride, force yourself
to suffer the faltering halt; that stalled freeze
before turning back; the sobbing, too,
you learned from your college dog who didn't "stay"
as you'd trained and trained him instead of yourself;
and the dead run your body hasn't known since childhood)
—her two boys, one a toddler, *alone*
for God's sake, asleep all by themselves
inside the house. What else could she do?
The husband is away—you guessed that,
of course, just as you knew it was the gate
someone left open as someone always does.

Her neighbors continue to look, but now, the loss
is yours, as well, because you cannot find
advice that doesn't ring of admonition,
consoling that isn't premature (it's been . . .
what? twelve minutes?), a single word to help
despite the fact that words are all you have,
that all you can do with one is to call it out,
time and again, as though it were a name,
and who- or whatever it belonged to
might hear it before your voice, too, gets lost
along with the dog, along with the rest
of a summer evening three hours brighter than your own.

But talk continues, knitting comfort from the slip
stitches of dialogue, as you recount
the time your dog escaped your parents . . . ,
or the leash that slipped . . . , and then that willful beagle—

when her dog bounds through the still-open
door to the deck (where it will remain for you,
memory being all that remains ajar),
muddies the kilim she couldn't care less about,
her blouse, her arms, and knocks the receiver to the floor.
Good boy, good boy, you hear the words chanted
because blame has been banished for all time,
because the dog's return has also returned
the dreams of two unknowing children upstairs,
the traveling husband who will rejoin her bed,
and even your own tiny voice on the floor
in the middle of the world, saying, *Let's talk tomorrow,*
because, really, it's there again, tomorrow,
just beyond the mullioned door and the gate
and the words that call the ones you love inside.

Sighting

I see their faces—those of friends departed
before their hearts had worn out this world's
brief welcome:

one squinting among the crowd that exits
a movie, one the moment someone lowers
the morning paper

to turn the page in a similitude of flight,
one on the aisle's other side at a wedding.
I catch a glimpse

that, like the wince of déjà vu, is but
my mind's own havoc—a record before
a recognition.

I see *their* faces (not resemblances),
which remind me not of their irreplaceable,
irrepressible

selves, or the chasm that others might bridge
though none could fill—but that which we call
spirits are simply

the earthly habits we keep: sightings of
our own missed selves, revenants
of how we have loved.

Haiku, Autumn

paw paw fruit
(Asimina triloba)

bare windbreak of elms
between neighbors, ignorant
that they stand as one

in one shaft of light,
on one strand of spider silk,
gold leaf winds . . . unwinds

branch-strewn, leaf-smothered,
after windstorms, all the paths
I know are you, trees

toe of my orange boot
kicking green black walnuts straight
into October

dawn's thick frost tangles
in cobwebs—not that there's a
spider to notice

how long have you hiked
with me, oak leaf, rain-glued to
my left boot's instep?

sailing air's current
elm leaf's crescent of sunlight
docks on its shadow

below hickories
nuts ping through leafy baffles—
minutes pass this way

how can oaks still hold
clouds of yellow when each gust
drenches us again

a week away, woods,
and you turned autumn—I don't
remember aging

under the dog's chase
umber leaves repeat their fall
flying up again

morning's first hard freeze
the pond gives up its last warmth
fog is summer's ghost

frost-coated spider web
various fallen leaves

Once Upon a Trail

Before our feet entered the woods,
somewhere and anywhere
shared the same address: nowhere
that had seen the likes of us.

And nowhere wondered where we were.

Before there was a trail in the woods,
every day was the same today.
No one stood around waiting
for tomorrow to arrive—now

was all that anything needed to do.

The woods was a place to stay, not go.
There wasn't a door that led elsewhere.
There wasn't a fence or lock for keeping
something in or something out—

we'd have been welcomed, had we arrived.

The feet that scrambled across its ground,
the feet that burrowed beneath it,
the feet that scurried high above it—
each saw the woods as perfect,

complete without a thought from us.

Until we arrived, when a tree fell,
the food and shade and harbor it held
above were simply offered to others
below: the worms and beetles and mice . . .

and no one thought: That tree must move.

But when we entered the woods, our eyes,
as if they were the eyelets of our boots,
saw nothing but rocks and roots to trip us,
rotted trunks to straddle, brambles

to snag us, mud to make us slip.

Everything blocked the way from where
we stood to where we wanted to be,
from here to there: two places
that had never existed before,

that made no sense to anyone but us.

When we entered the woods we brought
what none before had imagined:
change. Where we saw tangles of thorns,
nooses of vines, poison ivies,

stinging nettles, a webbing of weeds—
an utterly impassible place
where even the lowest limbs and saplings
seemed resolved to block our way—

we imagined a clearing, a trail.

Before this trail, we walked in circles,
we zigzagged, we lost our way,
we focused on what might lasso our feet,
scratch or net our faces in webs—

we never saw the trees for the forest.

And then, one day, we bring a spool,
tie it around a single trunk,
and weave a string among the woods—
from here to where a there might be:

a trail we want the woods to learn.

With pruners and loppers and saws, we slice
the fallen limbs and rotted trunks,
snip away whatever hangs or stands
or meanders in our way—

a way the land has never known.

With mower and rake, we sheer a path
that snakes across the woods, dividing
not just the woods, but the world, into halves—
left and right, far and near—

one on either side of a trail.

And now, even with friends and dogs,
we can walk the trail and see
what we've never seen before:
a single tree that isn't "Woods"

or "Forest" or *"Watch Your Head!"* Now,

There's a Pignut Hickory.
Here's a Pin Oak and a Dogwood.
And *those*, with leaves as long as a foot,
are Pawpaws, one day, to pick.

The woods no longer shares a name.

So now our boots can walk the carpet
we've mown and raked, our steps can come
like breaths, almost without thinking—
and now the woods is populated

with all the life we've never seen.

Yet now when a tree falls,
it blocks our trail. Do we keep
this promise to our path or break it?
No creature cares but us.

This trail, we may keep it up—

still, it is hardly ours to keep.
After our feet leave the woods,
somewhere and anywhere will share
the same address again, and nowhere

will recall the likes of us.

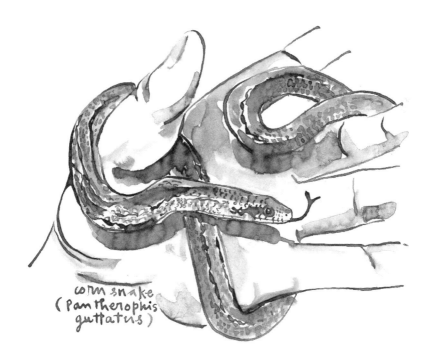

corn snake
(Pantherophis
guttatus)

Acknowledgments

My gratitude extends to the following editors and journals for publishing the following poems, some in earlier versions.

Prairie Schooner / "Georgic: On Apples"

Oxford Magazine / "On Hearing That, 2,000 Miles Away, Your Friend's Dog Has Just Run Off"

Southwest Review / "Georgic: On Japanese Beetles"

The Yale Review / "Sighting"

The Paris Review / "Georgic: On Your Nature"

Witness / "Blind"; "Georgic: On Spinning"

Western Humanities Review / "Georgic: On Soybeans"

Notre Dame Review / "Passers-by"

Salmagundi / "Totem"; "Georgic: On Varmints"

Diagram / "Georgic: On Blood"; "Georgic on Living Fences"

Knockout / "Georgic: On Firewood"; "Georgic: On Brooding"

Word 67, The School of Visual Arts / "A Knock Upon the Senses"; "On Still Reflections" (under the title "Kingfisher")

"Georgic: On a Redwood" appears on the audio CD *Writers' Block Party*, edited by Amy Krouse Rosenthal (Writers' Block Party, LLC, 2001). It is also included in *Cap City Poets*, an anthology (Pudding House Publications, 2008).

"Morel Season" appears in *Decomposition: An Anthology of Fungi-Inspired Poems*, edited by Renée Roehl and Kelly Chadwick (Lost Horse Press, 2010).